# The Huge Book of Fun Facts

by
Jake Jacobs

* * * * *

Published by Jake Jacobs

# 80.

McLane's legacy is honored through various landmarks and institutions named after him, including McLane Stadium at Baylor University in Texas.

# 81.

He is remembered as a true patriot and a dedicated servant of the American people.

# 82.

McLane's contributions to the founding of the United States and his commitment to the principles of liberty and justice continue to inspire generations.

# 83.

He believed in the power of education and was a strong advocate for the establishment of public schools.

# 84.

McLane was a firm believer in the importance of civic engagement and encouraged active participation in democratic processes.

# 85.

He was a skilled orator and used his eloquence to mobilize public support for important causes.

# 86.

McLane was deeply committed to preserving the ideals of the American Revolution and ensuring that future generations would benefit from the hard-fought freedoms.

# 87.

He actively participated in the political debates of his time, engaging in discussions on issues such as constitutional rights, economic policies, and foreign relations.

## 88.

McLane was a firm believer in the separation of powers and worked tirelessly to uphold the principles of checks and balances.

## 89.

He was a strong advocate for the protection of individual rights and fought against any encroachment on personal liberties.

## 90.

McLane's legal expertise made him a sought-after advisor in matters of constitutional interpretation and legislative drafting.

## 91.

He played a key role in the drafting of the Delaware Constitution of 1831, which incorporated many of the principles of the original U.S. Constitution.

## 92.

McLane's commitment to justice and equality extended to his involvement in legal cases involving civil rights and human rights.

## 93.

He provided pro bono legal representation to individuals facing discrimination and fought for equal treatment under the law.

## 94.

McLane's dedication to public service extended beyond his political career, as he actively supported charitable organizations and community initiatives.

## 95.

He believed in the importance of philanthropy and worked to improve the lives of the less fortunate.

## 96.

McLane's passion for social justice and equality led him to advocate for reforms in areas such as criminal justice, education, and healthcare.

## 97.

He was a proponent of progressive taxation and believed in the responsibility of the wealthy to contribute to the well-being of society.

## 98.

McLane's commitment to fairness and equity guided his decisions and actions throughout his life.

## 99.

He recognized the importance of diplomacy in international relations and worked to foster peaceful resolutions to conflicts.

## 100.

McLane's legacy is remembered not only for his political achievements but also for his unwavering dedication to the principles of justice, equality, and democracy.

## 101.

Thomas McKean (1734-1817) was an American lawyer, politician, and signer of the Declaration of Independence.

## 102.

Born in Pennsylvania, McKean studied law and became a prominent attorney in Delaware.

# 103.

He was known for his sharp legal mind and persuasive oratory skills.

# 104.

McKean served as a delegate to the Continental Congress from 1774 to 1783.

# 105.

He played a crucial role in shaping the policies and legislation of the early United States.

# 106.

McKean was a strong advocate for independence and was one of the signers of the Declaration of Independence in 1776.

# 107.

He served as the President of the Continental Congress from 1781 to 1782.

# 108.

McKean played a significant role in the drafting and ratification of the United States Constitution.

# 109.

He served as the Chief Justice of Pennsylvania from 1777 to 1799, making him one of the longest-serving justices in the state's history.

# 110.

McKean was known for his strict interpretation of the law and his commitment to upholding the principles of justice.

# 111.

# 158.

The significance of the rock art panels at Casa Malpais is still not fully understood, but they are believed to have had ceremonial and spiritual importance to the ancient inhabitants.

# 159.

Casa Malpais was likely a center for religious and ceremonial activities, with the Great Kiva serving as a focal point for communal rituals.

# 160.

The site was likely abandoned around the 14th century, and the reasons for its abandonment remain unknown.

# 161.

Casa Malpais was rediscovered by European settlers in the late 19th century, and archaeological excavations began in the early 20th century.

# 162.

Excavations at Casa Malpais have revealed a wealth of artifacts, including pottery, stone tools, and jewelry, providing valuable insights into the daily life and culture of the Mogollon people.

# 163.

The preservation of Casa Malpais is a challenge due to its exposed location and vulnerability to erosion and vandalism.

# 164.

Efforts have been made to protect and preserve the site, including the construction of a cover structure to shield the Great Kiva from the elements.

# 165.

Casa Malpais is listed on the National Register of Historic Places and is a designated National Historic Landmark.

# 166.

The site is open to the public, and guided tours are available to explore the pueblo complex and learn about its history and significance.

# 167.

Casa Malpais is considered one of the most important archaeological sites in the Southwest United States.

# 168.

The site offers visitors a unique opportunity to step back in time and experience the ancient culture of the Mogollon people.

# 169.

Casa Malpais has attracted the interest of archaeologists, historians, and anthropologists from around the world, who continue to study and learn from the site.

# 170.

The rock art at Casa Malpais has been a subject of artistic inspiration for contemporary Native American artists.

# 171.

Casa Malpais provides insights into the complex social, economic, and religious systems of the Mogollon culture.

# 172.

The site's location near the foothills of the White Mountains offers breathtaking views of the surrounding landscape.

# 173.

Casa Malpais is surrounded by a natural environment that is rich in biodiversity, with opportunities for wildlife viewing and outdoor exploration.

# 174.

The ancient pueblo walls at Casa Malpais stand as a testament to the ingenuity and craftsmanship of the Mogollon people.

# 175.

The site has served as an educational resource for local communities and schools, promoting a deeper understanding and appreciation of Native American history and culture.

# 176.

Casa Malpais is part of the larger Casa Malpais Archaeological Park, which includes interpretive trails and exhibits showcasing the site's significance.

# 177.

The Casa Malpais Visitor Center provides visitors with information about the site's history, guided tours, and educational programs.

# 178.

Casa Malpais has been the subject of ongoing research and archaeological investigations, uncovering new insights into its past.

# 179.

The site's location within the Apache-Sitgreaves National Forests offers opportunities for outdoor activities such as hiking, camping, and picnicking.

# 180.

Casa Malpais is a site of spiritual and cultural significance to Native American tribes in the region, who continue to maintain a connection to their ancestral lands.

# 181.

The preservation and interpretation of Casa Malpais is a collaborative effort involving federal agencies, tribal communities, and local stakeholders.

# 182.

The site has been used as a backdrop for cultural events and traditional ceremonies, fostering a connection between past and present generations.

# 183.

Casa Malpais serves as a reminder of the enduring legacy of the Native American peoples who once inhabited the area.

# 184.

The site's architectural features, such as the distinctive T-shaped doorways, reflect the unique artistic and cultural expressions of the Mogollon people.

# 185.

Casa Malpais provides opportunities for archaeological field schools and research projects, allowing students and scholars to gain hands-on experience in excavation and analysis.

# 186.

Mary Jane Colter was a renowned American architect and designer known for her work in the American Southwest.

# 187.

Colter's buildings are characterized by their integration with the natural landscape and their harmonious blend of traditional and contemporary architectural styles.

## 188.

Many of Colter's buildings were constructed in national parks and landmarks, including the Grand Canyon and the Desert View Watchtower.

## 189.

One of Colter's most famous creations is the Hopi House at the Grand Canyon, which was designed to resemble a traditional Hopi dwelling.

## 190.

The Hopi House features a distinctive stepped profile, adobe construction, and Native American-inspired decorations and artwork.

## 191.

Colter's buildings often incorporate elements of regional and indigenous architecture, paying homage to the cultural heritage of the Southwest.

## 192.

Colter's architectural style is often described as "National Park Rustic" or "Parkitecture" due to its close association with the natural environment and the national park system.

## 193.

Another notable work by Colter is the Desert View Watchtower, also located at the Grand Canyon. The tower's design was inspired by ancient Puebloan watchtowers and features panoramic views of the canyon.

## 194.

Colter was meticulous in her attention to detail, ensuring that every aspect of her buildings, from the overall design to the smallest decorative elements, contributed to the overall aesthetic and experience.

## 195.

Colter's buildings often reflect her deep appreciation for the Southwest's history, culture, and natural beauty.

## 196.

She collaborated closely with Native American artisans and craftsmen to incorporate their skills and traditions into her designs.

## 197.

Colter's buildings have become iconic symbols of the American Southwest, attracting visitors from around the world.

## 198.

The Lookout Studio, located near the Grand Canyon's Bright Angel Trailhead, is another notable creation by Colter. It offers stunning views of the canyon and blends seamlessly into its surroundings.

## 199.

Colter also designed the Phantom Ranch at the bottom of the Grand Canyon, providing a unique and remote lodging experience for adventurous travelers.

## 200.

The Hermit's Rest, a popular stopping point along the South Rim of the Grand Canyon, was also designed by Colter. Its rustic stone and timber construction creates a cozy and welcoming atmosphere.

## 201.

Colter's buildings often evoke a sense of nostalgia and romanticism, transporting visitors to a bygone era of exploration and adventure.

## 202.

Her designs were influenced by various architectural styles, including Spanish Colonial Revival, Pueblo Revival, and Arts and Crafts.

## 203.

Colter's attention to detail extended to the interior spaces of her buildings, where she carefully selected furnishings, artwork, and lighting to create a cohesive and immersive environment.

## 204.

Many of Colter's buildings feature large windows and open spaces to maximize natural light and provide breathtaking views of the surrounding landscapes.

## 205.

Colter's buildings are not only visually striking but also functional, designed to accommodate the needs of visitors while respecting the natural environment.

## 206.

The Watchtower at Desert View was designed with multiple levels, each providing a different perspective of the canyon and incorporating Native American-inspired artwork and murals.

## 207.

Colter's buildings are often cited as examples of sustainable architecture, as they were built using local materials and designed to blend harmoniously with the natural surroundings.

## 208.

Colter's designs were influenced by her extensive travels and study of architectural traditions around the world.

# 209.

Colter's buildings have inspired subsequent generations of architects and designers, who continue to draw inspiration from her innovative approach to blending architecture and nature.

# 210.

Despite being a woman in a predominantly male-dominated field, Colter gained recognition and respect for her unique architectural vision and contributions to the American Southwest.

# 211.

Colter's designs have stood the test of time, with many of her buildings still in use and appreciated by visitors today.

# 212.

The buildings designed by Colter are not just structures but gateways to experiencing the natural wonders and cultural richness of the Southwest.

# 213.

Colter's architectural designs prioritize the preservation of natural resources and seek to minimize the environmental impact of construction.

# 214.

The Hopi House at the Grand Canyon serves as both a museum and a gift shop, showcasing Native American artwork and crafts while providing a space for visitors to learn about the region's indigenous cultures.

# 215.

Arthur Middleton was born on June 26, 1742, in Middleton Place, South Carolina.

# 216.

He was born into a wealthy plantation-owning family and received a privileged upbringing.

# 217.

Middleton was well-educated and studied law at the Inns of Court in London.

# 218.

He returned to South Carolina and became actively involved in politics, advocating for the rights and liberties of the colonists.

# 219.

Middleton was a staunch supporter of American independence and played a key role in the Revolutionary War.

# 220.

He was elected to the Continental Congress and signed the Declaration of Independence on July 4, 1776.

# 221.

Middleton served in the Continental Army during the war and was captured by the British in 1780 during the Siege of Charleston.

# 222.

He was held as a prisoner of war for over a year until he was released in a prisoner exchange.

# 223.

Middleton was known for his strong leadership and persuasive speaking skills, which made him an influential figure in the Revolutionary movement.

# 224.

He was a proponent of religious freedom and played a significant role in drafting the South Carolina Constitution of 1778, which guaranteed religious liberty for all citizens.

## 225.

Middleton was also a strong advocate for education and helped establish the College of Charleston, which still exists today.

## 226.

After the war, Middleton served in various governmental positions, including as a state legislator and governor of South Carolina.

## 227.

He was a strong supporter of the newly formed United States and actively participated in shaping the nation's early political and legal institutions.

## 228.

Middleton was an avid supporter of agriculture and believed in the importance of improving farming practices and promoting economic growth.

## 229.

He was a dedicated family man and married Mary Izard in 1762. They had three children together.

## 230.

Middleton's plantation, known as Middleton Place, was one of the largest and most prosperous in South Carolina.

## 231.

He was an early advocate for the abolition of slavery and took steps to gradually emancipate the enslaved individuals on his plantation.

# 232.

Middleton was a respected horticulturist and played a significant role in the introduction and cultivation of various plant species in South Carolina.

# 233.

He was an active member of the Anglican Church and supported the construction of several churches in the region.

# 234.

Middleton was known for his elegant and refined taste in architecture, and Middleton Place showcases his architectural vision.

# 235.

He was passionate about preserving South Carolina's history and cultural heritage and was involved in the establishment of historical societies and preservation efforts.

# 236.

Middleton was a friend and correspondent of many prominent figures of the time, including Thomas Jefferson and George Washington.

# 237.

He was known for his diplomacy and negotiation skills, often mediating disputes and conflicts within the Revolutionary movement.

# 238.

Middleton's wealth allowed him to be a generous patron of the arts and sciences, supporting cultural endeavors in South Carolina.

# 239.

He was deeply committed to public service and believed in the importance of citizen participation in government.

## 240.

Middleton was well-regarded for his intelligence, integrity, and sense of fairness, which earned him the respect of his peers.

## 241.

He was a dedicated advocate for the rights of South Carolina and worked tirelessly to promote its interests at the national level.

## 242.

Middleton was an early proponent of economic independence and sought to develop South Carolina's industries and trade networks.

## 243.

He was known for his extensive library and collection of rare books, which showcased his intellectual curiosity and love for learning.

## 244.

Middleton played a significant role in the ratification of the United States Constitution and worked to ensure its adoption in South Carolina.

## 245.

He served as a judge and helped establish a fair and efficient legal system in the state.

## 246.

Middleton's contributions to the Revolutionary cause and the establishment of the United States were recognized and appreciated by his contemporaries.

## 247.

He believed in the power of education to uplift society and supported initiatives to expand access to education for all citizens.

## 248.

Middleton's political and legal writings continue to be studied and respected for their insights into the founding principles of the United States.

## 249.

He passed away on January 1, 1787, leaving behind a legacy of public service, intellectual curiosity, and dedication to the ideals of liberty and justice.

## 250.

James Monroe was born on April 28, 1758, in Westmoreland County, Virginia.

## 251.

He was the fifth President of the United States, serving from 1817 to 1825.

## 252.

Monroe was the last U.S. President who was a Founding Father and a participant in the American Revolution.

## 253.

He was a close friend and protégé of Thomas Jefferson and served as Jefferson's Minister to France from 1794 to 1796.

## 254.

Monroe played a crucial role in negotiating the Louisiana Purchase, which doubled the size of the United States.

## 255.

He also served as Secretary of State under President James Madison
and was instrumental in the drafting of the Monroe Doctrine.

## 256.

The Monroe Doctrine, announced in 1823, declared that the United
States would not tolerate European colonization or interference in
the Americas.

## 257.

Monroe is known for his presidency as the "Era of Good Feelings,"
characterized by political harmony and a sense of national unity.

## 258.

He was the last president to wear a powdered wig, as the fashion
changed during his term.

## 259.

Monroe was the first president to travel extensively during his
presidency, making a tour of the northern states and even visiting
military forts and Native American tribes.

## 260.

During his presidency, Monroe's administration oversaw the
acquisition of Florida from Spain through the Adams-Onís Treaty of
1819.

## 261.

He implemented protective tariffs to promote American industries
and supported internal improvements, such as roads and canals, to
stimulate economic growth.

## 262.

Monroe was the last president who was a veteran of the American
Revolutionary War.

## 263.

He was wounded in the Battle of Trenton during the Revolutionary War, becoming the last serving president to be injured in combat.

## 264.

Monroe was an advocate for the expansion of the United States and supported westward expansion and the admission of new states.

## 265.

He signed the Missouri Compromise in 1820, which allowed Missouri to enter the Union as a slave state while Maine entered as a free state, preserving the balance between slave and free states.

## 266.

Monroe was the only president to have two Secretaries of State— John Quincy Adams and John C. Calhoun—later becoming political rivals.

## 267.

He was the first president to ride on a steamboat, traveling on the Savannah in 1819.

## 268.

Monroe's presidency marked a period of territorial growth for the United States, with the acquisition of Florida, the Missouri Compromise, and various treaties with Native American tribes.

## 269.

He was an advocate for public education and supported the establishment of the University of Virginia.

## 270.

Monroe's presidency faced economic challenges, including the Panic of 1819, which led to a severe economic recession.

# 271.

He supported the construction of the Erie Canal, a major waterway that connected the Great Lakes to the Hudson River and facilitated trade and transportation.

# 272.

Monroe and his wife, Elizabeth Monroe, were known for their hospitality and elegant social gatherings at the White House.

# 273.

He was the last president to serve without a political party affiliation.

# 274.

Monroe had a deep respect for Native American tribes and believed in peaceful coexistence, although his policies regarding Native Americans were not always consistent.

# 275.

He was the first president to ride on a steam-powered train during his visit to the groundbreaking ceremony of the Baltimore and Ohio Railroad in 1828.

# 276.

Monroe served as a delegate to the Virginia Ratifying Convention, where he advocated for the adoption of the United States Constitution.

# 277.

He supported the expansion of the military and initiated the construction of coastal fortifications known as the "Monroe forts."

# 278.

Monroe's presidency witnessed the completion of the Erie Canal, which transformed transportation and trade between the eastern states and the Midwest.

## 279.

He promoted cultural and scientific exploration, including the Lewis and Clark Expedition and the establishment of a national botanical garden.

## 280.

Monroe is the only president to have been elected to office without any opposition in the Electoral College, receiving all but one electoral vote in the 1820 election.

## 281.

He established diplomatic relations with several Latin American countries and recognized their independence from European powers.

## 282.

Monroe had a keen interest in agriculture and owned a plantation in Virginia called Highland, where he experimented with new farming techniques.

## 283.

He was an avid reader and had an extensive personal library.

## 284.

Monroe's presidency saw the emergence of the "American System," an economic plan that aimed to promote industry, protect American manufacturers, and create a national bank.

## 285.

He was a strong advocate for a standing army and navy to protect the United States' interests at home and abroad.

## 286.

Monroe faced challenges with foreign policy, including tensions with Great Britain over maritime rights and conflicts with Native American tribes.

## 287.

He supported the construction of the Chesapeake and Ohio Canal, a planned transportation route connecting the Chesapeake Bay to the Ohio River.

## 288.

Monroe's presidency witnessed the first official visit by a reigning British monarch to the United States when King George IV visited in 1824.

## 289.

He was known for his calm and diplomatic demeanor, earning him the nickname "The Last Cocked Hat" for his distinctive style of dress.

## 290.

Monroe faced criticism for his handling of the Panic of 1819, with some accusing him of favoring wealthy interests over ordinary citizens.

## 291.

He implemented a naval blockade during the First Barbary War, which resulted in the end of tribute payments to Barbary states.

## 292.

Monroe served as Governor of Virginia from 1799 to 1802, during which he worked to modernize the state's infrastructure and promote economic development.

# 293.

He supported the construction of the National Road, a major highway project connecting the eastern states to the western frontier.

# 294.

Monroe's presidency saw the rise of the Monroeian Era, characterized by a sense of national pride and unity following the War of 1812.

# 295.

He was a strong advocate for a strong central government and believed in the importance of a strong military and a well-regulated militia.

# 296.

Monroe's presidency witnessed the beginning of the era of "Manifest Destiny," the belief that the United States was destined to expand its territory across the continent.

# 297.

He was the last president to have been born a British subject before the American Revolution.

# 298.

Monroe's presidency saw the emergence of the American Industrial Revolution, with significant advancements in manufacturing and transportation.

# 299.

He was a strong supporter of religious freedom and played a key role in the passage of the Virginia Statute for Religious Freedom, written by Thomas Jefferson.

# 300.

Monroe's presidency marked a transition in American politics from the early partisan divisions of the Federalist and Democratic-Republican parties to a more unified sense of nationalism and expansionism.

## 301.

The Australian Swiftlet, scientifically known as Aerodramus terraereginae, is a small bird species found in Australia, specifically in northern Queensland and the Torres Strait Islands.

## 302.

It is one of the smallest species of swiftlets, measuring about 10 centimeters in length.

## 303.

Australian Swiftlets have a unique flying pattern characterized by fast and agile flight, often seen in swirling flocks above forests and open areas.

## 304.

These birds have dark brown feathers with a glossy appearance, and their underparts are slightly paler in color.

## 305.

They have a short, rounded tail and pointed wings, which allow them to maneuver swiftly in flight.

## 306.

Australian Swiftlets are highly adapted to aerial life and spend most of their time in flight, even sleeping while flying.

## 307.

They are insectivorous birds, feeding on a variety of flying insects, such as beetles, ants, and termites, which they catch in mid-air using their wide beaks.

# 308.

These birds have a specialized gland called the salivary gland that produces a sticky saliva used to construct their nests.

# 309.

Australian Swiftlets build their nests using saliva and plant materials, attaching them to the walls of caves, cliffs, or man-made structures, such as buildings or bridges.

# 310.

The nests are small cup-shaped structures with a gelatinous texture, which hardens when exposed to air.

# 311.

The nests are highly prized in Chinese cuisine and are the primary ingredient in bird's nest soup, believed to have various health benefits.

# 312.

Australian Swiftlets are colonial birds, nesting in large groups or colonies with hundreds or even thousands of individuals.

# 313.

The colonies can be found in caves or other suitable nesting sites, creating a bustling and noisy environment.

# 314.

The breeding season of Australian Swiftlets usually occurs during the wet season when there is an abundance of insects for feeding their young.

# 315.

During courtship displays, male swiftlets perform aerial acrobatics, including high-speed dives, zigzag flight patterns, and vocalizations to attract females.

## 316.

After mating, the female Australian Swiftlet lays a single white egg in the nest, which both parents take turns incubating for about three weeks.

## 317.

The parents feed the hatchling with regurgitated insects until it is ready to fledge, which usually occurs around six weeks of age.

## 318.

Australian Swiftlets have a distinctive vocalization, producing a variety of calls and chirps, often heard during their aerial displays or while in the nesting colonies.

## 319.

These birds have a wide distribution across Australia, from the coastal regions to the inland areas, and are adaptable to a range of habitats.

## 320.

They are known to migrate seasonally, moving to different areas in search of food resources and suitable nesting sites.

## 321.

Australian Swiftlets are important for the ecosystem as they help control insect populations, contributing to the natural balance of their habitats.

## 322.

The population of Australian Swiftlets is considered stable and is not currently listed as a threatened species.

## 323.

They are protected by law in Australia, and it is illegal to disturb their nesting sites or collect their nests without proper permits.

## 324.

Australian Swiftlets are fascinating to researchers and scientists studying their flight patterns and navigational abilities.

## 325.

Their ability to navigate long distances and return to their nesting sites accurately is still not fully understood and continues to be the subject of scientific research.

## 326.

These birds have been known to undertake incredible migrations, covering hundreds of kilometers in a single day.

## 327.

Australian Swiftlets are also known to roost communally, gathering in large numbers at selected roosting sites, often near their nesting colonies.

## 328.

The communal roosting behavior serves multiple purposes, including protection from predators and social interaction.

## 329.

The conservation of suitable nesting and roosting sites is crucial for the long-term survival of Australian Swiftlets.

## 330.

They play a role in the pollination of plants by visiting flowers in search of nectar while foraging for insects.

# 331.

Australian Swiftlets have a relatively long lifespan, with individuals living up to 10 years or more in the wild.

# 332.

The presence of Australian Swiftlets in an area can indicate a healthy ecosystem with a diverse insect population.

# 333.

These birds have adapted to urban environments and can be found nesting in buildings and other man-made structures in cities.

# 334.

They are considered beneficial to humans as they help reduce the number of flying insects in urban areas.

# 335.

The nesting sites of Australian Swiftlets are often protected to ensure the preservation of their populations and the conservation of their unique nesting behavior.

# 336.

The sound of Australian Swiftlets' calls and the sight of their swift flight is a common feature of the Australian landscape, particularly in tropical and subtropical regions.

# 337.

Australian Swiftlets are highly social birds, and interactions between individuals within colonies are complex and structured.

# 338.

These birds communicate using a combination of vocalizations, visual displays, and physical contact.

# 339.

Australian Swiftlets have been observed engaging in cooperative behaviors, such as assisting in nest construction and defending nesting sites against intruders.

# 340.

They have well-developed eyesight, allowing them to navigate accurately during their fast and agile flight.

# 341.

Australian Swiftlets have been studied for their ability to sense and navigate using the Earth's magnetic field, a skill known as magnetoreception.

# 342.

The chicks of Australian Swiftlets are born naked and helpless, relying entirely on their parents for food and protection.

# 343.

The nests of Australian Swiftlets are often reused for multiple breeding seasons, with new layers of saliva and materials added each year.

# 344.

The swiftlets' nests are highly sought after in some cultures for their supposed medicinal and aphrodisiac properties.

# 345.

Australian Swiftlets are closely related to other species of swiftlets found in Southeast Asia, sharing similar behaviors and nesting habits.

# 346.

These birds have been studied for their unique adaptations to flight, providing valuable insights into avian physiology and aerodynamics.

## 347.

Australian Swiftlets are known to engage in "aerial mopping," where they fly close to water surfaces, collecting water droplets on their feathers to help with cooling.

## 348.

They are agile fliers and can change direction rapidly in mid-air, allowing them to catch insects with precision.

## 349.

Australian Swiftlets have a high metabolic rate, which enables them to sustain their active flight and foraging behaviors.

## 350.

They are fascinating examples of the diversity and adaptability of avian species, thriving in a range of habitats and environments across Australia.

## 351.

Bactrian camels (Camelus bactrianus) are large mammals native to the deserts of Central Asia, particularly Mongolia and China.

## 352.

They are distinct from their Arabian camel relatives, known as dromedaries, by having two humps instead of one.

## 353.

Bactrian camels are perfectly adapted to survive in harsh desert environments with extreme temperature fluctuations, ranging from scorching heat to freezing cold.

# 354.

The humps of Bactrian camels store fat, which they can metabolize and convert into energy and water during long periods without food or water.

# 355.

Adult Bactrian camels can weigh anywhere between 600 to 1,000 kilograms (1,320 to 2,200 pounds), with males generally being larger and heavier than females.

# 356.

Their humps can reach heights of up to 75 centimeters (30 inches) and are made of fatty tissue and fibrous connective tissue.

# 357.

Bactrian camels have a thick double-layered coat consisting of long outer guard hairs and a dense inner layer of wool, providing insulation against both cold and heat.

# 358.

The coat color of Bactrian camels varies, ranging from light tan to dark brown, allowing them to blend with the desert environment.

# 359.

They have long, powerful legs and broad, cushioned feet that enable them to walk on sandy and rocky terrain without sinking or causing damage to the delicate desert ecosystem.

# 360.

Bactrian camels have thick, bushy eyebrows and long, curved eyelashes that protect their eyes from sand and harsh winds.

# 361.

They have a tough leathery mouth that can withstand thorny vegetation, enabling them to feed on a wide variety of desert plants.

## 362.

Bactrian camels are herbivorous, primarily feeding on grasses, leaves, and desert shrubs, but they can also browse on thorny plants and dry vegetation.

## 363.

These camels have a unique chewing mechanism that allows them to extract maximum nutrients from tough and fibrous desert vegetation.

## 364.

Bactrian camels are well-known for their ability to go long periods without drinking water. They can survive for several weeks by relying on the water stored in their body fat and the moisture from the vegetation they consume.

## 365.

When water is available, Bactrian camels can drink up to 57 liters (15 gallons) in just 10 minutes, rapidly replenishing their water reserves.

## 366.

Bactrian camels have a remarkable tolerance for extreme temperatures, with the ability to withstand temperatures as low as -40 degrees Celsius (-40 degrees Fahrenheit) in winter and as high as 40 degrees Celsius (104 degrees Fahrenheit) in summer.

## 367.

They can tolerate low humidity levels, as their efficient kidneys help conserve water by producing highly concentrated urine and reducing water loss.

## 368.

Bactrian camels have a strong immune system and are less prone to diseases compared to other domesticated animals.

## 369.

They are well-adapted to walking long distances, capable of covering up to 40 kilometers (25 miles) in a day.

## 370.

Bactrian camels have been domesticated for over 4,000 years and have played a crucial role in the transportation of goods and people across the deserts of Central Asia.

## 371.

They were historically used as pack animals on the Silk Road, carrying goods such as silk, spices, and precious metals between Asia and Europe.

## 372.

Bactrian camels have a calm and docile temperament, making them suitable for handling and domestication.

## 373.

They have been selectively bred for different purposes, including meat, milk, and wool production, as well as transportation.

## 374.

The wool of Bactrian camels is highly prized for its quality and warmth. It is used to make textiles and garments in the regions where they are found.

## 375.

Bactrian camels have a long lifespan, with individuals living up to 40 years in captivity.

# 376.

They have a unique social structure, living in small family groups consisting of a dominant male, several females, and their offspring.

# 377.

The dominant male, known as a bull, establishes and defends his territory and harem of females.

# 378.

Bactrian camels communicate through a variety of vocalizations, including grunts, groans, and bellows, as well as non-verbal cues such as body postures and gestures.

# 379.

During the breeding season, males engage in aggressive displays, including neck wrestling and spitting, to establish dominance and win mating rights.

# 380.

Female Bactrian camels have a gestation period of around 13 months, giving birth to a single calf.

# 381.

Calves are born with a woolly coat and are able to walk shortly after birth.

# 382.

The mother provides milk to her calf for up to a year, after which the calf starts eating solid food.

# 383.

Bactrian camels have a strong bond with their offspring, and the mother is highly protective, defending her calf against predators and other threats.

# 384.

Predators of Bactrian camels include wolves, snow leopards, and bears.

# 385.

Bactrian camels have a strong sense of smell, allowing them to detect water sources from long distances.

# 386.

They have an innate sense of direction and are capable of finding their way back to familiar territories, even in the vast and featureless desert landscapes.

# 387.

Bactrian camels are often used as tourist attractions and can be ridden or used for camel trekking experiences in desert regions.

# 388.

They have a gentle and swaying gait, providing a unique and memorable riding experience.

# 389.

Bactrian camels have been introduced to other parts of the world, including Australia and the United States, where they are used for leisure activities and as attractions in zoos and wildlife parks.

# 390.

In their natural habitats, Bactrian camels are considered a vulnerable species due to habitat loss, overhunting, and competition with domestic livestock for resources.

# 391.

Conservation efforts are being made to protect and preserve wild Bactrian camel populations, including establishing protected areas and implementing sustainable management practices.

## 392.

Bactrian camels have become a symbol of resilience and adaptability, representing the harsh but beautiful landscapes of the Central Asian deserts.

## 393.

They have been featured in various forms of art, literature, and cultural traditions of the regions where they are found.

## 394.

Bactrian camels are known for their ability to store and retrieve memories of water sources, even after long periods of time.

## 395.

They have a specialized liver that helps them break down and process toxins found in certain plants, allowing them to consume a wider range of vegetation.

## 396.

Bactrian camels have been used in scientific research to study adaptations to extreme environments and to gain insights into their unique physiological and behavioral traits.

## 397.

The Bactrian camel is the largest mammal native to the deserts of Central Asia.

## 398.

Bactrian camels have a distinctive appearance, with their long, curved necks, large heads, and bushy eyebrows.

# 399.

They have powerful jaws and teeth that enable them to chew tough desert plants and extract nutrients efficiently.

# 400.

Bactrian camels are a culturally significant animal in the regions they inhabit, often associated with traditions, folklore, and nomadic lifestyles.

# 401.

The Desert Laboratory, also known as the Desert Botanical Laboratory, is a research facility located in Tucson, Arizona, United States.

# 402.

It was established in 1903 by the Carnegie Institution of Washington as a center for studying the unique desert ecosystems.

# 403.

The Desert Laboratory was one of the first research institutions dedicated to studying desert flora and fauna.

# 404.

Its primary focus is on the Sonoran Desert, one of the most biodiverse desert regions in the world.

# 405.

The laboratory sits on a 400-acre plot of land in the Tucson Mountains, providing researchers with access to diverse desert habitats.

# 406.

The Desert Laboratory has played a significant role in advancing our understanding of desert ecology, plant physiology, and adaptation to arid environments.

## 407.

Scientists at the laboratory conduct research on a wide range of topics, including plant anatomy, plant water relations, pollination, seed dispersal, and plant-animal interactions.

## 408.

The laboratory has contributed to the discovery and description of numerous plant and animal species found in the Sonoran Desert.

## 409.

It has also played a crucial role in documenting the effects of climate change and human activities on desert ecosystems.

## 410.

The Desert Laboratory houses a herbarium, which contains a vast collection of preserved plant specimens used for scientific study and reference.

## 411.

The laboratory's research findings have had practical applications in the fields of conservation, land management, and sustainable desert agriculture.

## 412.

The Desert Laboratory collaborates with other research institutions, universities, and government agencies to foster interdisciplinary research and knowledge exchange.

## 413.

The facility provides a platform for scientists, students, and professionals to conduct fieldwork, collect data, and study the desert environment.

## 414.

The Desert Laboratory offers educational programs and workshops to promote public awareness and understanding of desert ecosystems.

## 415.

It provides opportunities for students and researchers to engage in hands-on field research and gain practical experience in desert ecology.

## 416.

The laboratory's location in the Tucson Mountains offers breathtaking views of the surrounding desert landscape, providing inspiration and a conducive environment for research.

## 417.

Over the years, the Desert Laboratory has hosted renowned scientists and researchers who have made significant contributions to the field of desert ecology.

## 418.

The facility has a long-standing commitment to promoting conservation and sustainable use of desert resources.

## 419.

It actively participates in conservation initiatives aimed at protecting rare and endangered plant species in the Sonoran Desert.

## 420.

The Desert Laboratory conducts long-term monitoring projects to track changes in desert ecosystems and assess the impacts of environmental disturbances.

## 421.

The laboratory's researchers use advanced technologies and techniques, such as remote sensing, GIS mapping, and DNA analysis, to study desert plants and animals.

## 422.

It maintains a network of weather stations and data loggers to monitor climate patterns, rainfall, temperature, and other environmental factors.

## 423.

The Desert Laboratory has a library and archives that house a vast collection of scientific publications, books, and historical documents related to desert ecology.

## 424.

The facility has a visitor center where the public can learn about the research conducted at the laboratory and explore interactive exhibits on desert ecosystems.

## 425.

The Desert Laboratory has been designated as a National Historic Landmark, recognizing its historical and scientific significance.

## 426.

It has been the site of numerous influential studies and publications that have shaped the field of desert ecology.

## 427.

The Desert Laboratory has inspired the establishment of similar research institutions and conservation organizations focused on desert environments worldwide.

## 428.

The facility provides resources and expertise for desert restoration projects and the rehabilitation of degraded desert lands.

## 429.

The Desert Laboratory is home to a variety of plant and animal species, including cacti, desert wildflowers, reptiles, birds, and mammals.

## 430.

Researchers at the laboratory have made significant contributions to understanding the adaptations of desert plants to water scarcity, such as succulence, CAM photosynthesis, and deep root systems.

## 431.

The facility has contributed to the development of desert gardening techniques and the cultivation of drought-tolerant plants for landscaping purposes.

## 432.

The Desert Laboratory's research has shed light on the ecological role of desert animals, such as seed dispersal by rodents and the interactions between pollinators and desert flowers.

## 433.

The laboratory has a network of hiking trails and field stations that allow researchers to study different desert habitats and ecosystems.

## 434.

It conducts regular workshops and seminars on desert ecology, attracting scientists and researchers from around the world.

# 435.

The Desert Laboratory has been instrumental in developing best practices for managing invasive plant species in desert environments.

# 436.

The facility has an extensive database of plant and animal species found in the Sonoran Desert, which serves as a valuable resource for ecological studies.

# 437.

The Desert Laboratory's researchers collaborate with indigenous communities to document traditional ecological knowledge and promote culturally sensitive conservation practices.

# 438.

The facility conducts outreach programs to schools and local communities, raising awareness about the importance of desert ecosystems and the need for their conservation.

# 439.

The Desert Laboratory has contributed to the development of guidelines for sustainable tourism and recreational activities in desert areas.

# 440.

It maintains a seed bank, preserving the genetic diversity of desert plant species and providing a resource for habitat restoration projects.

# 441.

The Desert Laboratory hosts field courses and training programs for students and professionals interested in studying desert ecology and conservation.

# 442.

The facility has state-of-the-art laboratories and research facilities equipped with specialized equipment for studying desert plants and animals.

# 443.

The Desert Laboratory has played a crucial role in advocating for the protection of desert lands and influencing land-use policies in the region.

# 444.

The facility collaborates with botanic gardens and arboretums to exchange plant specimens, seeds, and knowledge for conservation and research purposes.

# 445.

The Desert Laboratory has contributed to the development of sustainable farming practices in arid regions, including techniques for water conservation and soil management.

# 446.

The facility provides support for citizen science projects, encouraging the public to participate in data collection and monitoring efforts in the desert.

# 447.

The Desert Laboratory's research has provided insights into the potential use of desert plants for medicinal and pharmaceutical purposes.

# 448.

It has documented the ecological relationships between desert plants and their insect pollinators, highlighting the importance of preserving biodiversity for ecosystem stability.

# 449.

The facility hosts scientific conferences and symposiums focused on desert ecology, bringing together researchers and experts from diverse disciplines.

# 450.

The Desert Laboratory continues to be a leading institution for desert research, contributing to our understanding of these unique and fragile ecosystems.

# 451.

El Tovar was built in 1905 and is considered one of the premier historic hotels in the United States.

# 452.

It was designed by architect Charles Whittlesey in the rustic style of the Arts and Crafts movement.

# 453.

El Tovar was named after Spanish explorer Don Pedro de Tovar, who was part of Francisco Vázquez de Coronado's expedition in the 16th century.

# 454.

The hotel's location provides breathtaking views of the Grand Canyon.

# 455.

El Tovar is situated just steps away from the rim of the canyon, making it a popular destination for tourists.

# 456.

The hotel features a unique blend of rustic elegance and Old West charm.

## 457.

El Tovar was originally built as a luxury hotel to accommodate tourists visiting the Grand Canyon.

## 458.

It has welcomed many notable guests throughout history, including Theodore Roosevelt, Albert Einstein, and Bill Clinton.

## 459.

The hotel's lobby showcases a grand fireplace made of limestone and showcases Native American artwork.

## 460.

El Tovar has been designated as a National Historic Landmark.

## 461.

The hotel offers a variety of rooms, including standard rooms, suites, and cabins.

## 462.

Many of the rooms at El Tovar feature stunning views of the canyon.

## 463.

The hotel's dining room offers a gourmet menu with a focus on regional and sustainable ingredients.

## 464.

El Tovar's dining room is known for its elegant atmosphere and panoramic views of the canyon.

## 465.

The hotel has a gift shop where visitors can purchase unique souvenirs and Native American artwork.

## 466.

El Tovar has its own ice cream parlor, offering a sweet treat for guests.

## 467.

The hotel offers guided tours of the Grand Canyon for guests who want to explore the area.

## 468.

El Tovar has a long-standing tradition of exceptional service and hospitality.

## 469.

The hotel's architecture and design are inspired by the natural surroundings and Native American culture.

## 470.

El Tovar has been featured in several films and television shows, including "National Lampoon's Vacation."

## 471.

The hotel's location provides access to numerous hiking trails and outdoor activities in the Grand Canyon National Park.

## 472.

El Tovar has been featured in many photographs and artwork depicting the beauty of the Grand Canyon.

## 473.

The hotel's historic charm and unique location make it a popular venue for weddings and special events.

# 474.

El Tovar offers a range of amenities for guests, including a fitness center and concierge services.

# 475.

The hotel has a rich history and has been a witness to the changing landscape and development of the Grand Canyon.

# 476.

El Tovar has played a significant role in promoting tourism to the Grand Canyon and preserving its natural beauty.

# 477.

The hotel has undergone several renovations and upgrades throughout the years to ensure guest comfort and satisfaction.

# 478.

El Tovar has a dedicated staff that is knowledgeable about the area and can provide information and recommendations to guests.

# 479.

The hotel's proximity to the Grand Canyon allows guests to experience the stunning sunrise and sunset views over the canyon.

# 480.

El Tovar is open year-round, allowing visitors to experience the beauty of the Grand Canyon in all seasons.

# 481.

The hotel offers a shuttle service for guests who want to explore different areas of the Grand Canyon.

# 482.

El Tovar has a cozy lounge where guests can relax and enjoy a drink while taking in the magnificent views.

## 483.

The hotel's architecture reflects the regional materials and natural elements found in the Grand Canyon area.

## 484.

El Tovar is known for its high-quality service and attention to detail.

## 485.

The hotel's location provides opportunities for wildlife viewing, with the chance to see deer, elk, and various bird species.

## 486.

El Tovar has a long-standing commitment to sustainability and has implemented various eco-friendly practices.

## 487.

The hotel has received numerous awards and accolades for its exceptional service and hospitality.

## 488.

El Tovar is a popular destination for artists and photographers looking to capture the beauty of the Grand Canyon.

## 489.

The hotel offers special packages and promotions throughout the year, including seasonal discounts and holiday packages.

## 490.

El Tovar has a rich collection of historical photographs and artifacts on display, showcasing the hotel's heritage.

# 491.

The hotel's location provides easy access to the Grand Canyon Village, where visitors can find additional amenities and attractions.

# 492.

El Tovar has a cozy reading room where guests can unwind with a book or enjoy the view.

# 493.

The hotel has a dedicated team of guides and experts who offer educational programs and presentations on the Grand Canyon's history and geology.

# 494.

El Tovar has a rich culinary tradition, with a focus on using local and sustainable ingredients.

# 495.

The hotel's dining room offers a variety of menu options, including vegetarian and gluten-free choices.

# 496.

El Tovar has a wine cellar that features a diverse selection of wines from around the world.

# 497.

The hotel hosts special events and themed dinners throughout the year, showcasing the culinary talents of its chefs.

# 498.

El Tovar is located near several popular hiking trails, including the Bright Angel Trail and the South Kaibab Trail.

# 499.

The hotel's location provides opportunities for stargazing, with clear night skies and minimal light pollution.

## 500.

El Tovar has a rich cultural heritage, with a deep appreciation for the Native American tribes that have inhabited the Grand Canyon region for centuries.

## 501.

Lewis Morris was born on April 8, 1726, in Morrisania, New York, into a prominent family.

## 502.

He was the son of Lewis Morris Sr., the first Lord of the Manor of Morrisania, and a wealthy landowner.

## 503.

Morris received a classical education and studied law, becoming a successful lawyer.

## 504.

He was a member of the prominent Morris family, which played a significant role in colonial and early American history.

## 505.

Morris was a staunch supporter of American independence and played a key role in the American Revolution.

## 506.

He was a delegate from New York to the Continental Congress, serving from 1775 to 1777.

## 507.

Morris signed the United States Declaration of Independence in 1776, representing the state of New York.

## 508.

He was one of the wealthiest men in the American colonies and used his resources to support the patriot cause.

## 509.

Morris served as a brigadier general in the New York militia during the Revolutionary War.

## 510.

He played a crucial role in the defense of New York City during the British invasion in 1776.

## 511.

Morris's estate in the Bronx, known as Morrisania, was confiscated by the British during the war.

## 512.

After the war, Morris was elected to the New York State Assembly and served from 1777 to 1781.

## 513.

He played a significant role in drafting the New York State Constitution in 1777.

## 514.

Morris was appointed as a judge on the New York Supreme Court in 1779.

## 515.

He served as a delegate to the Annapolis Convention in 1786, which laid the groundwork for the Constitutional Convention.

# 516.

Morris was a strong advocate for a strong central government and supported the ratification of the United States Constitution.

# 517.

He was elected to the United States Senate from New York and served from 1789 to 1790.

# 518.

Morris resigned from the Senate due to health reasons and returned to his private life.

# 519.

He continued to be involved in public affairs and served as a presidential elector in 1796 and 1800.

# 520.

Morris was an early advocate for the abolition of slavery and emancipated the slaves on his estate during his lifetime.

# 521.

He played a role in the development of infrastructure in New York, including advocating for the construction of the Erie Canal.

# 522.

Morris was a prominent landowner and played a key role in the development of Westchester County, New York.

# 523.

He was a founding member of the New York Society for the Promotion of Agriculture, Arts, and Manufactures.

# 524.

Morris was known for his hospitality and entertained many prominent figures of his time at his estate.

## 525.

He was a close friend and correspondent of George Washington and Thomas Jefferson.

## 526.

Morris was a member of the Society of the Cincinnati, an organization founded by officers of the Revolutionary War.

## 527.

He had a passion for horticulture and maintained extensive gardens on his estate.

## 528.

Morris had a strong interest in education and served as a trustee for various educational institutions.

## 529.

He supported the establishment of a national university and served as a trustee for the College of New Jersey (now Princeton University).

## 530.

Morris was an active participant in the cultural and intellectual life of his time, engaging in scientific and philosophical discussions.

## 531.

He was an avid reader and collector of books, amassing a substantial library.

## 532.

Morris was a patron of the arts and supported local artists and craftsmen.

## 533.

He had a deep appreciation for nature and enjoyed outdoor activities such as hunting and fishing.

## 534.

Morris was known for his integrity and honesty, earning the respect and trust of his peers.

## 535.

He had a strong sense of civic duty and actively participated in public service throughout his life.

## 536.

Morris's contributions to the early United States were recognized and celebrated by his contemporaries.

## 537.

He was considered one of the leading statesmen of his time and was respected for his wisdom and judgment.

## 538.

Morris passed away on January 22, 1798, at the age of 71, at his estate in Morrisania.

## 539.

He was buried in the family vault at St. Ann's Episcopal Church in the Bronx.

## 540.

Morris's legacy is remembered through various landmarks and institutions named after him, including Morrisania in the Bronx and Morris County in New Jersey.

# 541.

His former estate, Morrisania, is now part of the Bronx and is a neighborhood with a rich history.

# 542.

Morris's contributions to the American Revolution are commemorated at the Lewis Morris Park in the Bronx, which features a monument dedicated to him.

# 543.

Several portraits of Lewis Morris are housed in museums and historical societies, preserving his likeness for future generations.

# 544.

Morris's life and contributions are documented in various historical records and publications, providing insights into his role in shaping American history.

# 545.

He was a dedicated public servant who worked tirelessly to advance the principles of liberty and independence.

# 546.

Morris's commitment to the American cause and his dedication to public service make him an important figure in American history.

# 547.

His participation in the Continental Congress and his signing of the Declaration of Independence demonstrate his commitment to the ideals of the American Revolution.

# 548.

Morris's legal expertise and his role in shaping the New York State Constitution highlight his contributions to the legal framework of the newly formed nation.

## 549.

His advocacy for a strong central government and his involvement in the ratification of the United States Constitution reflect his vision for a united and prosperous nation.

## 550.

Lewis Morris's life and accomplishments serve as a reminder of the courage, sacrifice, and dedication of the Founding Fathers in establishing the United States of America.

## 551.

Robert Morris was born on January 20, 1734, in Liverpool, England, and later immigrated to the American colonies.

## 552.

He settled in Philadelphia, Pennsylvania, where he became a successful merchant and financier.

## 553.

Morris played a vital role in financing the American Revolution and was known as the "Financier of the Revolution."

## 554.

He served as a delegate to the Continental Congress from 1775 to 1778 and again from 1781 to 1784.

## 555.

Morris was a signer of the United States Declaration of Independence in 1776, representing Pennsylvania.

# 556.

He served on various congressional committees, including the Committee of Secret Correspondence and the Committee of Commerce.

# 557.

Morris advocated for the establishment of a strong central government and was influential in the drafting of the United States Constitution.

# 558.

He played a key role in the creation of the Bank of North America, the first federally-chartered bank in the United States.

# 559.

Morris served as the Superintendent of Finance from 1781 to 1784, overseeing the financial operations of the newly formed United States government.

# 560.

He was instrumental in stabilizing the nation's finances and implementing policies to address the Revolutionary War debt.

# 561.

Morris personally financed a significant portion of the war effort, using his own wealth and credit to support the cause.

# 562.

He provided financial assistance to General George Washington and the Continental Army, helping to sustain their operations.

# 563.

Morris's financial acumen and business connections made him a trusted advisor to Washington and other prominent figures of the time.

## 564.

He was a strong advocate for the establishment of a national mint and the adoption of a decimal currency system.

## 565.

Morris's financial difficulties after the war, including bankruptcy, led to his imprisonment for debt from 1798 to 1801.

## 566.

Despite his personal setbacks, Morris continued to be involved in public service and philanthropic endeavors.

## 567.

He played a role in the development of infrastructure, including promoting canal construction and the improvement of transportation routes.

## 568.

Morris was a strong supporter of education and served as a trustee for the University of Pennsylvania.

## 569.

He was an early proponent of prison reform, advocating for humane treatment of prisoners and their rehabilitation.

## 570.

Morris had an interest in scientific exploration and supported several scientific expeditions, including those led by John Bartram.

## 571.

He had a keen interest in agriculture and horticulture, promoting the cultivation of new crops and the improvement of farming practices.

## 572.

Morris was a member of the Society of the Cincinnati, an organization formed by Revolutionary War officers.

## 573.

He was known for his elegant and extravagant lifestyle, displaying wealth and success through his opulent residences and possessions.

## 574.

Morris's home, known as the Morris Mansion, was a grand estate in Philadelphia that hosted influential figures of the time.

## 575.

He had a strong sense of public duty and actively participated in community affairs and civic organizations.

## 576.

Morris's personal library was extensive, reflecting his intellectual curiosity and love for learning.

## 577.

He corresponded with many notable figures of the time, including George Washington, Thomas Jefferson, and Benjamin Franklin.

## 578.

Morris's business ventures extended beyond the United States, and he was involved in international trade and commerce.

## 579.

He played a significant role in negotiating trade treaties with European countries, including the Treaty of Amity and Commerce with France.

## 580.

Morris was a supporter of the abolition of slavery and took steps to gradually emancipate the enslaved individuals on his properties.

## 581.

He served as a United States Senator from Pennsylvania from 1789 to 1795.

## 582.

Morris was one of the wealthiest men in America during his time, but his financial difficulties later in life tarnished his reputation.

## 583.

He died on May 8, 1806, in Philadelphia at the age of 72.

## 584.

Morris's contributions to the United States were recognized and celebrated by his contemporaries, who considered him a founding father.

## 585.

He left a lasting legacy in American history as a financial and political leader during the nation's formative years.

## 586.

Morris County, New Jersey, is named in his honor, as well as various streets, buildings, and institutions across the country.

## 587.

The Robert Morris University in Pittsburgh, Pennsylvania, is named after him and continues to educate students in his legacy.

## 588.

Several portraits and sculptures of Robert Morris can be found in museums and historical institutions, preserving his image for future generations.

## 589.

His life and accomplishments are documented in numerous historical records, biographies, and scholarly works.

## 590.

Morris's business acumen and financial expertise continue to be studied and admired by economists and historians.

## 591.

He was a visionary leader who understood the importance of economic stability and fiscal responsibility in building a nation.

## 592.

Morris's financial strategies and policies helped establish a strong foundation for the young United States.

## 593.

He had a reputation for being level-headed, practical, and resourceful, qualities that served him well in his financial endeavors.

## 594.

Morris's contributions to the American Revolution were essential in sustaining the war effort and ensuring the success of the patriot cause.

## 595.

He was deeply committed to the principles of liberty, independence, and self-governance.

## 596.

Morris's advocacy for a strong central government helped shape the structure and functions of the early United States government.

## 597.

His efforts to establish a national banking system and promote sound financial practices laid the groundwork for future economic development.

## 598.

Morris's role in drafting and ratifying the United States Constitution cemented his position as a key figure in the nation's founding.

## 599.

He believed in the power of commerce and trade to drive economic growth and create prosperity for the American people.

## 600.

Robert Morris's life and achievements exemplify the spirit of entrepreneurship, innovation, and public service that shaped the early years of the United States of America.

## 601.

Badgers are small to medium-sized mammals belonging to the Mustelidae family, which also includes weasels, otters, and ferrets.

## 602.

There are 11 different species of badgers, including the European badger, American badger, and honey badger.

## 603.

Badgers are found in various habitats around the world, including grasslands, woodlands, and deserts.

# 604.

They have a distinct body shape with a stocky build, short legs, and a long, low body.

# 605.

Badgers are known for their powerful digging abilities and use their long claws to excavate burrows and search for food.

# 606.

They are primarily nocturnal animals, being most active during the night.

# 607.

Badgers are omnivorous and have a varied diet that includes insects, small mammals, birds, fruits, and roots.

# 608.

They have a keen sense of smell and use it to locate prey and detect predators.

# 609.

Badgers have a characteristic black and white striped face, which is different in pattern for each species.

# 610.

They have a thick, coarse fur that helps them withstand harsh weather conditions.

# 611.

Badgers are solitary animals and usually live alone or in small family groups.

# 612.

They are generally territorial and mark their territories with scent markings.

# 613.

Badgers are known for their strong jaws and teeth, which they use to crush the shells of their prey.

# 614.

They are excellent swimmers and can cross rivers and other bodies of water with ease.

# 615.

Badgers are not aggressive but can be fierce when provoked or defending their territory.

# 616.

They have a distinctive vocalization called a "churring" sound, which they use to communicate with other badgers.

# 617.

Badgers are known for their strong sense of loyalty to their family members and will defend them if necessary.

# 618.

They have a lifespan of around 10 to 15 years in the wild, although some species can live longer in captivity.

# 619.

Badgers are adaptable animals and can survive in a wide range of environments.

# 620.

They are important ecosystem engineers, as their digging activities create burrows that provide shelter for other animals.

## 621.

Badgers play a vital role in controlling rodent populations by preying on mice, rats, and other small mammals.

## 622.

They have a unique method of hunting called "sit-and-wait" predation, where they patiently wait near burrow entrances for their prey to emerge.

## 623.

Badgers have a remarkable ability to dig tunnels and burrows, often reaching several meters in length.

## 624.

They are known to have a symbiotic relationship with some bird species, such as the European roller and the honeyguide bird, which lead them to termite nests for a shared meal.

## 625.

Badgers are well-known for their thick skin, which provides protection against bites and scratches during fights with other animals.

## 626.

They have a keen sense of hearing and can detect low-frequency sounds that are inaudible to humans.

## 627.

Badgers are often associated with wisdom, tenacity, and determination in folklore and mythology.

# 628.

They have been depicted in various forms of art, literature, and popular culture, including children's books such as "The Wind in the Willows."

# 629.

Badgers are known to create multiple entrances and exits to their burrows, providing escape routes in case of danger.

# 630.

They are meticulous groomers and spend a significant amount of time cleaning their fur and removing parasites.

# 631.

Badgers have a slow metabolic rate, allowing them to conserve energy during periods of inactivity.

# 632.

They are resistant to snake venom and are known to prey on venomous snakes such as rattlesnakes and adders.

# 633.

Badgers are highly adaptable to changing environments and can thrive in both rural and urban areas.

# 634.

They have a relatively low reproductive rate, with females giving birth to one to five cubs in a litter.

# 635.

Badger cubs, also called kits, stay with their mother until they are about six months old before venturing out on their own.

# 636.

They have a unique mating ritual that involves scent marking and vocalizations to attract potential mates.

## 637.

Badgers have a strong sense of direction and can navigate long distances using landmarks and scent trails.

## 638.

They have a hinged lower jaw that allows them to open their mouths wide when capturing prey or defending themselves.

## 639.

Badgers are known to exhibit playful behavior, engaging in mock fights and chasing each other.

## 640.

They are highly sensitive to disturbances in their environment and can be easily stressed by human activities.

## 641.

Badgers have a well-developed sense of touch, particularly in their front paws, which they use for digging and manipulating objects.

## 642.

They are known for their strong bond with their burrows and will defend them fiercely against intruders.

## 643.

Badgers have a keen sense of balance and are capable of climbing trees and navigating uneven terrain.

## 644.

They have a remarkable ability to adapt to different climates, ranging from hot deserts to cold mountainous regions.

# 645.

Badgers are social animals and engage in mutual grooming with other members of their group as a form of bonding.

# 646.

They have a relatively low body temperature, allowing them to conserve energy in cold environments.

# 647.

Badgers are highly intelligent animals and can learn complex tasks and problem-solving techniques.

# 648.

They have a specialized adaptation called a nictitating membrane, which is a transparent eyelid that protects their eyes while digging.

# 649.

Badgers have been hunted for their fur in the past, leading to a decline in their populations in certain regions.

# 650.

They are protected by laws in many countries and are recognized as important contributors to biodiversity and ecosystem health.

# 651.

The Baltimore Oriole (Icterus galbula) is a species of songbird belonging to the family Icteridae.

# 652.

It is named after the colors of Lord Baltimore, who were associated with orange and black.

# 653.

Baltimore Orioles are native to North America and are primarily found in the eastern and central regions of the United States and southern Canada.

## 654.

They are migratory birds and spend their winters in southern Florida, Central America, and the Caribbean.

## 655.

Male Baltimore Orioles are known for their vibrant orange plumage with black wings, tail, and throat.

## 656.

Females have a more muted coloration, with yellowish-orange underparts and grayish-brown upperparts.

## 657.

Orioles have a distinctive and melodious song that consists of clear whistles and rich, flute-like notes.

## 658.

They build elaborate hanging nests, often referred to as "pouch nests," which are woven from plant fibers and suspended from the branches of trees.

## 659.

Baltimore Orioles are skilled weavers, using a technique called "basket weaving" to create their nests.

## 660.

The female oriole is the primary nest builder, while the male assists in gathering materials.

## 661.

Their nests are typically located in tall deciduous trees, providing protection from predators.

## 662.

Orioles have a preference for open woodlands, forest edges, and gardens, where they can find a variety of fruits, nectar, and insects.

## 663.

They have a specialized brush-like tongue that allows them to feed on nectar from flowers.

## 664.

Orioles are also known to eat insects, spiders, berries, and other small fruits.

## 665.

They play an essential role in pollination as they visit flowers in search of nectar.

## 666.

Baltimore Orioles are highly territorial during the breeding season and defend their nesting territory from intruders.

## 667.

Males display courtship behavior by singing and flapping their wings to attract females.

## 668.

Once a pair bond is established, both male and female Orioles participate in nest building and raising the young.

## 669.

Females typically lay 3-7 eggs per clutch, and both parents take turns incubating the eggs.

# 670.

The incubation period lasts about 12-14 days, and the chicks fledge after approximately 12-14 days.

# 671.

Orioles are known for their agility and acrobatic flight patterns, making them a delight to watch.

# 672.

They are social birds and often gather in small flocks during migration and in communal roosts during the winter months.

# 673.

Baltimore Orioles are known to engage in "anting," where they rub ants on their feathers, possibly to rid themselves of parasites.

# 674.

Their populations have been impacted by habitat loss due to deforestation and urbanization.

# 675.

Orioles are highly susceptible to collisions with glass windows and structures, and efforts have been made to promote bird-friendly architecture.

# 676.

Orioles are sometimes attracted to backyard feeders that offer oranges, grape jelly, and sugar water.

# 677.

They are generally monogamous and mate with the same partner each breeding season.

# 678.

Orioles are known to engage in aggressive behaviors to protect their territory and young from predators.

# 679.

They have a diverse range of vocalizations, including calls, chatters, and alarm notes.

# 680.

The average lifespan of Baltimore Orioles is around 5-6 years, although some individuals have been known to live longer.

# 681.

Orioles are occasionally parasitized by brown-headed cowbirds, which lay their eggs in the oriole's nest for the orioles to raise.

# 682.

The Baltimore Oriole is the state bird of Maryland.

# 683.

The species has been featured on postage stamps in the United States and Canada.

# 684.

Baltimore Orioles are known to migrate at night, using celestial cues and the Earth's magnetic field for navigation.

# 685.

They are not closely related to the true orioles of the Old World but share a similar appearance and behavior.

# 686.

Orioles are known to engage in "gaping" behavior, where they pry open flowers to access nectar deep inside.

# 687.

They are important seed dispersers, as they consume fruits and then excrete the undigested seeds in different locations.

# 688.

Orioles have a strong beak that they use for piercing fruits and probing for insects.

# 689.

They are known to defend their nests vigorously against potential predators, including snakes, squirrels, and birds of prey.

# 690.

Orioles are highly vocal during the breeding season but tend to be quieter during migration and winter.

# 691.

The oldest recorded Baltimore Oriole in the wild lived to be at least 11 years and 4 months old.

# 692.

The Baltimore Oriole's scientific name, Icterus galbula, is derived from the Greek words "ikteros," meaning yellow, and "galbula," meaning greenish-yellow.

# 693.

The song of the Baltimore Oriole is often described as a "liquid whistle" and can be heard from a considerable distance.

# 694.

Orioles have been known to imitate the songs of other bird species, adding a variety of calls to their repertoire.

# 695.

They have a keen sense of hearing and can detect subtle sounds and calls from their surroundings.

# 696.

Orioles have excellent eyesight, allowing them to spot small prey and navigate through dense foliage.

# 697.

They are agile climbers and can move adeptly through trees and branches.

# 698.

Orioles are often associated with the arrival of spring and are considered harbingers of the season.

# 699.

The vibrant colors of the male Baltimore Oriole's plumage serve as a form of courtship display to attract females.

# 700.

Orioles are considered charismatic birds and are enjoyed by birdwatchers and nature enthusiasts for their beauty and song.

# 701.

Fort Huachuca is a United States Army installation located in Cochise County, Arizona.

# 702.

It is situated in the Huachuca Mountains near the town of Sierra Vista.

# 703.

The name "Huachuca" is derived from a Native American word meaning "place of thunder."

## 704.

Fort Huachuca was established in March 1877 to provide protection for settlers and transportation routes in the region.

## 705.

It has a rich history and played a significant role in the Indian Wars, the Apache Wars, and World War II.

## 706.

The fort served as the headquarters for the 10th Cavalry, an African American unit known as the "Buffalo Soldiers."

## 707.

The Buffalo Soldiers were instrumental in maintaining peace and protecting settlers in the area.

## 708.

Fort Huachuca was a major training center during World War II, where soldiers received specialized intelligence and signal training.

## 709.

The fort is known as the "Home of Military Intelligence," as it has been the primary intelligence training center for the U.S. Army since 1954.

## 710.

The U.S. Army Intelligence Center and the U.S. Army Network Enterprise Technology Command are both located at Fort Huachuca.

## 711.

The fort covers an area of approximately 73,000 acres, making it one of the largest military installations in Arizona.

## 712.

Fort Huachuca is situated at an elevation of around 5,000 feet, providing a moderate climate throughout the year.

## 713.

The installation is surrounded by diverse natural landscapes, including deserts, mountains, and canyons.

## 714.

The fort's location in southeastern Arizona provides strategic proximity to the U.S.-Mexico border and allows for realistic training in a variety of environments.

## 715.

The fort has a museum, the Fort Huachuca Museum, which showcases the history and heritage of the installation and the U.S. Army in the region.

## 716.

Fort Huachuca is home to the U.S. Army Garrison, which provides support services and infrastructure for soldiers and their families stationed there.

## 717.

The fort employs a significant civilian workforce, contributing to the local economy and community.

## 718.

The installation is a hub for military communications, intelligence gathering, and cybersecurity operations.

# 719.

Fort Huachuca hosts various training courses and programs, including military intelligence, electronic warfare, and network operations.

# 720.

The fort has an active partnership with nearby universities and educational institutions, promoting academic and research collaborations.

# 721.

Fort Huachuca has a robust wildlife management program, with efforts to protect and preserve the diverse plant and animal species in the area.

# 722.

The installation provides recreational opportunities for soldiers and their families, including hiking, camping, and fishing.

# 723.

The Buffalo Corral Riding Stables at Fort Huachuca offer horseback riding and equestrian activities.

# 724.

The fort has its own golf course, the Mountain View Golf Course, which is open to military personnel and the public.

# 725.

Fort Huachuca has a diverse cultural heritage, with historical sites, museums, and events that celebrate the region's history and Native American traditions.

# 726.

The post cemetery at Fort Huachuca is the final resting place for soldiers and their families, including many Buffalo Soldiers.

## 727.

The fort has been recognized for its efforts in environmental sustainability and resource conservation.

## 728.

The installation has its own fire and emergency services department, ensuring the safety and security of personnel and facilities.

## 729.

Fort Huachuca has a close-knit community, with a range of support services and activities for military families.

## 730.

The installation hosts various events throughout the year, including ceremonies, parades, and community gatherings.

## 731.

Fort Huachuca is a designated National Historic Landmark, recognizing its historical significance and contributions to the nation.

## 732.

The fort has a strong partnership with the local community, fostering positive relationships and mutual support.

## 733.

The installation is home to the Buffalo Soldier Memorial, honoring the service and sacrifice of the African American soldiers who served at Fort Huachuca.

## 734.

Fort Huachuca has its own post exchange, commissary, and other amenities to meet the needs of military personnel and their families.

## 735.

The fort's location in southern Arizona offers stunning views of the surrounding mountain ranges and picturesque landscapes.

## 736.

Fort Huachuca has a robust training infrastructure, including firing ranges, simulation facilities, and tactical training areas.

## 737.

The fort has its own medical clinic and hospital, providing healthcare services for military personnel and their dependents.

## 738.

Fort Huachuca supports various community outreach programs, including volunteering, mentorship, and educational initiatives.

## 739.

The installation has its own chapels and religious services to accommodate the diverse spiritual needs of personnel.

## 740.

Fort Huachuca is located near several national parks and recreational areas, allowing for outdoor adventures and exploration.

## 741.

The fort has a strong emphasis on physical fitness, with gyms, sports fields, and fitness programs available for soldiers and their families.

## 742.

Fort Huachuca has its own military police and security forces, ensuring the safety and well-being of personnel and facilities.

# 743.

The installation has a dedicated Family Readiness Center, providing support services and resources for military families.

# 744.

Fort Huachuca has a strong commitment to diversity and inclusion, fostering an environment of respect and equality.

# 745.

The fort has a historical reenactment group, the Buffalo Soldiers of Arizona Territory, which educates the public about the history and legacy of the Buffalo Soldiers.

# 746.

Fort Huachuca hosts regular ceremonies and events to honor fallen soldiers and recognize outstanding achievements.

# 747.

The installation offers educational opportunities through its on-base schools and partnerships with local educational institutions.

# 748.

Fort Huachuca has its own veterinary clinic, providing healthcare services for military working dogs and pets.

# 749.

The fort has its own legal services office, offering assistance and guidance to military personnel and their families.

# 750.

Fort Huachuca is an integral part of the U.S. Army's mission to provide national defense and ensure the readiness of its forces.

# 751.

The Grand Canyon Depot is a historic train station located near the South Rim of the Grand Canyon in Arizona, USA.

# 752.

It was designed by architect Francis W. Wilson and constructed in 1909-1910.

# 753.

The depot was built to serve the passengers of the Atchison, Topeka, and Santa Fe Railway.

# 754.

It is a prime example of the Rustic Style of architecture, blending harmoniously with the natural surroundings.

# 755.

The building features a unique combination of stone, wood, and log construction.

# 756.

The depot's design was inspired by the Swiss chalet style, with a sloping roof, wide eaves, and decorative woodwork.

# 757.

It is one of the few remaining original structures in the Grand Canyon Village.

# 758.

The depot served as a gateway to the Grand Canyon for tourists arriving by train.

# 759.

The train station played a crucial role in the development of tourism at the Grand Canyon.

## 760.

It facilitated the transportation of visitors from distant cities, making the canyon more accessible.

## 761.

The depot served as a hub for passenger arrivals and departures, with ticketing offices, waiting rooms, and baggage facilities.

## 762.

It also housed a Western Union telegraph office, providing communication services to visitors and railway personnel.

## 763.

The depot's location near the rim allowed for convenient access to the Grand Canyon's scenic viewpoints.

## 764.

The iconic El Tovar Hotel, another historic landmark, is situated adjacent to the depot.

## 765.

The depot's construction materials were sourced locally, using stones and timbers from the surrounding area.

## 766.

It was added to the National Register of Historic Places in 1974.

## 767.

The depot continues to serve as an active train station, with daily passenger service provided by the Grand Canyon Railway.

## 768.

Visitors can board the vintage steam-powered train at the depot and enjoy a scenic journey to the Grand Canyon.

## 769.

The depot's interior features rustic wood paneling, large windows, and a cozy fireplace.

## 770.

The waiting room displays historical photographs and artifacts, providing a glimpse into the area's rich railroad history.

## 771.

The depot's architecture and location make it a popular subject for photographers and artists.

## 772.

It is often depicted in paintings and photographs capturing the grandeur of the Grand Canyon.

## 773.

The depot has been featured in several movies and TV shows, adding to its cultural significance.

## 774.

It serves as a symbol of the golden age of rail travel and the exploration of the American West.

## 775.

The depot's strategic location near the rim allows visitors to disembark from the train and immediately experience the awe-inspiring views.

## 776.

The building's log and stone construction helps it blend harmoniously with the natural environment.

## 777.

The depot's design reflects the influence of the Arts and Crafts movement, which sought to integrate architecture with nature.

## 778.

The depot has undergone restoration and preservation efforts over the years to maintain its original charm.

## 779.

It serves as a reminder of the early days of tourism at the Grand Canyon and the importance of rail transportation.

## 780.

The depot's architecture has influenced the design of other structures in the Grand Canyon Village.

## 781.

It stands as a testament to the craftsmanship and architectural ingenuity of its time.

## 782.

The depot's location near the historic Bright Angel Trailhead allows for convenient access to hiking trails.

## 783.

The depot is often bustling with activity, as visitors and tourists arrive and depart throughout the day.

## 784.

It serves as a gathering point for those embarking on their Grand Canyon adventure.

# 785.

The depot's distinctive appearance makes it a recognizable landmark in the Grand Canyon Village.

# 786.

The depot's proximity to other historic sites, such as the Kolb Studio and Hopi House, enhances its cultural significance.

# 787.

The depot's exterior features intricate woodwork and decorative elements that add to its charm.

# 788.

It serves as a meeting point for guided tours and organized activities within the park.

# 789.

The depot's architecture reflects the vision of its designer, Francis W. Wilson, to create a structure that complements the surrounding landscape.

# 790.

The depot has witnessed significant historical events, including the arrival of influential figures and the growth of tourism.

# 791.

It serves as a reminder of the role that rail travel played in opening up the American West to exploration and settlement.

# 792.

The depot's covered platform provides shelter for passengers waiting for the train.

# 793.

The depot has a close relationship with the nearby Grand Canyon National Park, working in harmony to enhance the visitor experience.

# 794.

It serves as a gateway to the natural wonders of the Grand Canyon, welcoming visitors from around the world.

# 795.

The depot's location near the rim allows for stunning panoramic views of the canyon's vastness.

# 796.

The depot's surroundings are landscaped with native plants, further integrating it with the natural environment.

# 797.

The depot's historical significance is celebrated through interpretive displays and exhibits inside the building.

# 798.

It is a popular spot for visitors to take commemorative photos before or after their Grand Canyon exploration.

# 799.

The depot's architectural details, such as the exposed beams and decorative brackets, add to its visual appeal.

# 800.

The depot's continued operation ensures that the spirit of the railroad era lives on at the Grand Canyon.

# 801.

John Morton was born on April 20, 1725, in Ridley Township, Pennsylvania.

## 802.

He was an American colonial politician and a signer of the Declaration of Independence.

## 803.

Morton's family emigrated from Sweden to Pennsylvania in the late 1600s.

## 804.

He was educated at the Latin School in Philadelphia and later studied law.

## 805.

Morton served as a justice of the peace and a member of the Pennsylvania Provincial Assembly.

## 806.

He played a crucial role in Pennsylvania's resistance to British rule leading up to the American Revolution.

## 807.

Morton was elected to the Continental Congress in 1774 and attended all sessions until his death.

## 808.

He was a strong advocate for independence and was one of the Pennsylvania delegates who signed the Declaration of Independence on July 4, 1776.

## 809.

Morton was known for his careful consideration and thoughtful approach to legislative matters.

## 810.

He played a key role in securing Pennsylvania's support for the Declaration of Independence.

## 811.

Morton was instrumental in the drafting of the Articles of Confederation, the first constitution of the United States.

## 812.

He served on various congressional committees, including the Committee of Secret Correspondence and the Committee of Safety.

## 813.

Morton was known for his strong belief in representative government and the principles of liberty and equality.

## 814.

He was a member of the moderate faction in Congress, advocating for a balanced approach in dealing with British oppression.

## 815.

Morton was among the delegates who signed the United States Constitution in 1787.

## 816.

He served as the chairman of the Pennsylvania delegation during the ratification process.

## 817.

Morton was elected to the Pennsylvania House of Representatives in 1776 and served as speaker from 1780 to 1782.

# 818.

He was appointed to the Pennsylvania Supreme Executive Council in 1784 and served as vice president of the council.

# 819.

Morton's health began to decline in the late 1780s, affecting his political activities.

# 820.

He died on April 1, 1777, in Ridley Township, Pennsylvania, at the age of 51.

# 821.

Morton's grave is located at St. Paul's Episcopal Churchyard in Chester, Pennsylvania.

# 822.

He is remembered as one of the Founding Fathers of the United States, having played a significant role in shaping the nation's early years.

# 823.

Morton's signature on the Declaration of Independence is considered one of the most distinctive and elaborate.

# 824.

He is the only signer of the Declaration of Independence buried in Pennsylvania.

# 825.

Morton's contributions to the American Revolution and the formation of the United States are commemorated in various historical markers and memorials.

# 826.

In 1976, a commemorative postage stamp featuring John Morton was issued as part of the Bicentennial Series.

# 827.

The John Morton Homestead, his former residence in Ridley Township, is now a historic site.

# 828.

Morton's political career was marked by his dedication to public service and his commitment to the ideals of liberty and self-governance.

# 829.

He was known for his integrity and his ability to bridge different factions for the greater good.

# 830.

Morton's efforts helped shape Pennsylvania's political landscape and establish its commitment to independence.

# 831.

His decision to support independence despite personal risks demonstrated his unwavering dedication to the cause.

# 832.

Morton's influence extended beyond Pennsylvania, as he played a part in shaping the nation's early political institutions.

# 833.

He was respected among his peers for his wisdom, intellect, and commitment to the principles of the American Revolution.

# 834.

Morton's legacy as a signer of the Declaration of Independence continues to inspire and educate future generations.

# 835.

His contributions to the birth of the nation are recognized and celebrated as a vital part of American history.

# 836.

Morton's work helped establish the foundations of American democracy and laid the groundwork for future generations of leaders.

# 837.

He is often referred to as one of Pennsylvania's most influential political figures of the Revolutionary era.

# 838.

Morton's commitment to the principles of freedom and equality set an example for future leaders and citizens.

# 839.

His legacy serves as a reminder of the sacrifices and dedication of those who fought for American independence.

# 840.

Morton's name is included among the other signers of the Declaration of Independence on the National Mall in Washington, D.C.

# 841.

His role as a representative of Pennsylvania in the Continental Congress reflects his state's significant contribution to the American Revolution.

## 842.

Morton's commitment to public service and the ideals of the American Revolution make him a revered figure in American history.

## 843.

He is often mentioned alongside other Founding Fathers as a key figure in the nation's founding.

## 844.

Morton's legacy extends beyond his political career, as his ideals and principles continue to shape American society.

## 845.

His contributions to the development of the United States as an independent nation cannot be overstated.

## 846.

Morton's story is a testament to the courage and determination of the individuals who fought for American liberty.

## 847.

His willingness to put his life and reputation on the line for the cause of independence showcases his unwavering commitment.

## 848.

Morton's impact on American history is not only significant but also enduring.

## 849.

His name and contributions are remembered and celebrated in historical books, museums, and educational materials.

# 850.

Morton's life and achievements serve as a reminder of the importance of individual action and dedication to the principles of liberty and self-government.

# 851.

The Bean Goose (Anser fabalis) is a species of migratory goose that belongs to the family Anatidae.

# 852.

It is also known as the Tundra Bean Goose or Eurasian Bean Goose.

# 853.

Bean Geese are large birds, measuring about 27 to 33 inches (70 to 84 cm) in length and weighing around 5 to 9 pounds (2.3 to 4 kg).

# 854.

They have a wingspan of approximately 5 to 6 feet (1.5 to 1.8 meters).

# 855.

The plumage of the Bean Goose varies depending on the subspecies but is generally gray-brown in color.

# 856.

They have a distinctive orange or pinkish bill with a black base.

# 857.

Bean Geese have short, pink legs and webbed feet.

# 858.

The species is highly migratory, breeding in the northern regions of Europe and Asia and wintering in southern parts of Europe, Asia, and Africa.

# 859.

During migration, Bean Geese form large flocks that can number in the thousands.

# 860.

Their migration routes can span thousands of miles, with some populations traveling from as far as Arctic Russia to wintering grounds in Western Europe.

# 861.

Bean Geese are primarily herbivorous and feed on a variety of plant matter, including grasses, sedges, and aquatic vegetation.

# 862.

They also consume grains, seeds, and berries when available.

# 863.

Bean Geese are known to forage in agricultural fields, wetlands, and coastal areas.

# 864.

During the breeding season, Bean Geese nest in wetland areas such as marshes, bogs, and tundra habitats.

# 865.

They construct nests from vegetation and line them with down feathers for insulation.

# 866.

Female Bean Geese typically lay a clutch of 4 to 7 eggs, which are incubated by both parents for about 25 to 30 days.

# 867.

The hatchlings, called goslings, are precocial and can swim and feed themselves shortly after hatching.

## 868.

Bean Geese are monogamous and form long-term pair bonds, often mating for life.

## 869.

They communicate through a variety of vocalizations, including honks, cackles, and hisses.

## 870.

Bean Geese are known for their V-shaped flying formations during migration, which help conserve energy and facilitate navigation.

## 871.

They are highly social birds and often gather in large flocks during the non-breeding season.

## 872.

Bean Geese have been observed engaging in courtship displays, including head bowing and wing flapping.

## 873.

The lifespan of Bean Geese in the wild is estimated to be around 10 to 15 years.

## 874.

They face several threats in their natural habitats, including habitat loss, hunting, and pollution.

## 875.

The International Union for Conservation of Nature (IUCN) classifies the Bean Goose as a species of "Least Concern" in terms of conservation status.

# 876.

However, certain subspecies of the Bean Goose, such as the Taiga Bean Goose, are listed as "Vulnerable" due to population decline.

# 877.

Bean Geese are protected under various international conservation agreements, such as the African-Eurasian Migratory Waterbird Agreement (AEWA).

# 878.

The species has a wide range and can be found across several countries, including Russia, Scandinavia, China, Japan, and parts of Europe.

# 879.

In some regions, Bean Geese are considered a game species and are hunted legally during designated hunting seasons.

# 880.

Bean Geese are highly adapted to their cold, Arctic breeding habitats, with specialized feathers and fat reserves to withstand extreme temperatures.

# 881.

They have a complex digestive system that allows them to efficiently extract nutrients from plant material.

# 882.

Bean Geese are known to undergo molting, during which they shed and replace their feathers.

# 883.

They are excellent swimmers and are often found in or near water bodies.

# 884.

Bean Geese have a strong flight and can cover long distances during migration.

# 885.

The species has a close genetic relationship with other goose species, such as the Pink-footed Goose and the White-fronted Goose.

# 886.

Bean Geese are not typically kept in captivity, as they require large open spaces for their natural behaviors.

# 887.

However, they are occasionally seen in zoos or bird sanctuaries as part of conservation breeding programs or educational displays.

# 888.

Bean Geese are known to interact with other bird species, including ducks, swans, and other geese, during their migration and wintering periods.

# 889.

They have been observed forming mixed-species flocks, which provide safety in numbers and facilitate information exchange.

# 890.

Bean Geese have a strong sense of orientation and can navigate using celestial cues, landmarks, and the Earth's magnetic field.

# 891.

The species is well-studied by ornithologists and has contributed to our understanding of bird migration patterns and behavior.

## 892.

Bean Geese play a vital ecological role in their habitats by dispersing seeds and fertilizing vegetation through their droppings.

## 893.

They are known to exhibit social hierarchy within their flocks, with dominant individuals having access to preferred feeding areas.

## 894.

Bean Geese have been featured in various cultural and artistic depictions, including paintings, literature, and folklore.

## 895.

The species has inspired conservation efforts to protect their breeding and wintering habitats.

## 896.

Bean Geese are highly adaptable and can utilize a range of wetland and grassland habitats for feeding and nesting.

## 897.

They have a distinctive flight call, which is often described as a loud, honking sound.

## 898.

Bean Geese are closely related to domestic geese and can hybridize with certain domestic breeds.

## 899.

The presence of Bean Geese in an area can indicate the ecological health and richness of wetland habitats.

# 900.

Birdwatchers and nature enthusiasts consider seeing a flock of Bean Geese during migration a remarkable and memorable experience.

# 901.

Beetles belong to the order Coleoptera, which is the largest order of insects, comprising over 400,000 known species.

# 902.

They can be found in nearly every habitat on Earth, from forests and grasslands to deserts and freshwater ecosystems.

# 903.

Beetles come in a wide variety of sizes, ranging from the tiny featherwing beetles that measure only 0.3 mm to the formidable titan beetle, which can grow up to 6.5 inches long.

# 904.

The exoskeleton of beetles is made of a tough, chitinous substance that provides protection and support.

# 905.

Beetles have two pairs of wings: the forewings, known as elytra, which are usually hard and shell-like, and the hindwings, which are used for flight.

# 906.

When at rest, beetles fold their hindwings beneath the elytra, creating a protective covering.

# 907.

Some beetles have evolved modified elytra that allow them to fly with the wings exposed, such as the bombardier beetle.

# 908.

Beetles exhibit incredible diversity in terms of shape, color, and pattern. They can be shiny, iridescent, metallic, or camouflaged to blend with their surroundings.

# 909.

Many beetles are herbivores and feed on plants, while others are predatory, scavengers, or parasitic.

# 910.

The diet of beetles can include leaves, wood, nectar, pollen, fruits, fungi, other insects, carrion, and even blood.

# 911.

Some beetles are specialized pollinators, playing a crucial role in plant reproduction and ecosystem balance.

# 912.

Beetles have a complete metamorphosis lifecycle, including egg, larva, pupa, and adult stages.

# 913.

Beetle larvae, often called grubs or caterpillars, are specialized for their specific habitats and diets.

# 914.

Larvae may live in the soil, wood, water, or other substrates, depending on the species.

# 915.

The length of the larval stage can vary greatly, lasting from a few weeks to several years, depending on environmental conditions and species.

# 916.

Beetle larvae undergo a process called pupation, during which they transform into the adult form inside a protective casing called a pupa.

# 917.

The pupal stage is a period of development and metamorphosis.

# 918.

Beetle adults have specialized mouthparts adapted to their specific diets. They may have chewing mouthparts for herbivory or piercing-sucking mouthparts for feeding on fluids.

# 919.

Many beetles have powerful jaws that allow them to crush and consume tough plant material or prey.

# 920.

Beetles have compound eyes, which are made up of multiple lenses that enable them to detect movement and perceive their surroundings.

# 921.

Some beetle species have incredible vision, capable of perceiving ultraviolet light or polarized light.

# 922.

Beetles also have a pair of antennae that help them detect chemicals, air movements, and other sensory cues.

# 923.

The lifespan of beetles varies widely among species, ranging from a few weeks to several years.

# 924.

Some beetles exhibit parental care, with adults guarding eggs or providing food for their larvae.

# 925.

Many beetles have unique defense mechanisms to protect themselves from predators. These can include chemical defenses, camouflage, mimicry, and playing dead.

# 926.

The bombardier beetle is famous for its ability to produce and spray a hot chemical mixture from its abdomen when threatened.

# 927.

Some beetles, such as the fireflies, produce bioluminescence, which they use for communication and courtship.

# 928.

Beetles have been around for millions of years, with fossil evidence dating back over 300 million years.

# 929.

They have survived mass extinction events and have adapted to various environmental changes.

# 930.

Some beetles are considered pests, damaging crops, stored food, or wooden structures.

# 931.

However, beetles also provide important ecological services, such as pollination, nutrient cycling, and decomposition.

# 932.

Some beetles, like the dung beetles, play a vital role in recycling animal waste and maintaining ecosystem health.

# 933.

Certain beetle species have cultural and symbolic significance in different societies and religions.

# 934.

In ancient Egypt, the scarab beetle was revered as a symbol of rebirth and regeneration.

# 935.

Beetle fossils have provided valuable insights into the evolution and history of Earth's ecosystems.

# 936.

The study of beetles, known as coleopterology, is a popular field of entomology.

# 937.

Beetles are often collected and studied by amateur entomologists and beetle enthusiasts.

# 938.

Some beetles, such as ladybugs and stag beetles, are popular and beloved by people due to their colorful appearance and perceived good luck.

# 939.

Beetles can be found on every continent except Antarctica.

# 940.

The smallest beetle in the world, Nanosella fungi, measures just 0.25 mm long.

## 941.

The largest beetle in terms of weight is the Goliath beetle, which can weigh up to 3.5 ounces (100 grams).

## 942.

The Goliath beetle is also one of the heaviest insects in the world.

## 943.

The longest beetle is the titan beetle, which can reach lengths of over 6.5 inches (16.7 cm).

## 944.

Some beetles are excellent climbers and can traverse vertical surfaces, such as the wall-climbing robot inspired by the leaf beetle.

## 945.

Beetles play a role in scientific research and have contributed to advancements in fields such as biomimicry, materials science, and genetics.

## 946.

Beetles are sensitive to environmental changes and can serve as indicators of habitat health and pollution.

## 947.

The intricate and diverse anatomy of beetles has fascinated scientists and artists alike, leading to detailed illustrations and sculptures.

## 948.

Beetles have been featured in literature, folklore, and popular culture throughout history.

# 949.

They are often depicted as symbols of strength, resilience, transformation, and adaptability.

# 950.

The study of beetles continues to uncover new species, behaviors, and ecological interactions, highlighting the remarkable diversity and importance of this insect group.

# 951.

Grand Canyon Village is located on the South Rim of the Grand Canyon in Arizona, USA.

# 952.

It is the main hub for tourism and visitor services at the Grand Canyon National Park.

# 953.

The village was established in 1901 as the first developed area within the park.

# 954.

It sits at an elevation of approximately 6,800 feet (2,073 meters) above sea level.

# 955.

The village offers stunning panoramic views of the Grand Canyon, attracting millions of visitors each year.

# 956.

It is home to iconic structures such as the El Tovar Hotel, Hopi House, and Bright Angel Lodge.

# 957.

El Tovar Hotel, built in 1905, is a historic and luxurious hotel known for its rustic charm and breathtaking views.

# 958.

Hopi House, designed by architect Mary Colter, showcases Native American arts and crafts and offers a glimpse into Hopi culture.

# 959.

Bright Angel Lodge, built in 1935, provides lodging, dining, and access to the Bright Angel Trail.

# 960.

The village offers a range of accommodations, including hotels, lodges, cabins, and campgrounds, catering to different budgets and preferences.

# 961.

It is a designated National Historic Landmark District.

# 962.

The village serves as a starting point for various hiking trails, including the popular Bright Angel Trail and South Kaibab Trail.

# 963.

The historic Grand Canyon Railway, which operates a scenic train ride from Williams, Arizona, terminates at the Grand Canyon Depot in the village.

# 964.

The village is home to several restaurants, cafes, and gift shops where visitors can enjoy meals, snacks, and souvenirs.

# 965.

The Grand Canyon Visitor Center, located in the village, provides information, exhibits, and ranger-led programs to enhance visitors' understanding of the park.

## 966.

Mule rides, offered by the Grand Canyon Trail Rides, allow visitors to explore the canyon from a unique perspective.

## 967.

The village has a post office, bank, grocery store, and other essential services to cater to both visitors and residents.

## 968.

The Grand Canyon Association, a nonprofit organization, operates bookstores and visitor centers within the village, supporting educational and preservation efforts.

## 969.

The Grand Canyon Clinic, located in the village, provides medical services for visitors and park employees.

## 970.

Grand Canyon Village has a rich history and has witnessed significant development over the years while preserving its natural and cultural heritage.

## 971.

The village offers shuttle services to various points of interest within the park, reducing traffic congestion and promoting sustainability.

## 972.

It hosts special events and cultural programs throughout the year, including art exhibits, music performances, and ranger-led talks.

# 973.

The Kolb Studio, perched on the canyon rim, showcases the work of pioneering photographers Ellsworth and Emery Kolb.

# 974.

The village provides access to stunning sunrise and sunset views, offering breathtaking colors and shadows over the canyon.

# 975.

It is a popular spot for stargazing, offering dark skies and excellent visibility of celestial objects.

# 976.

The village is surrounded by diverse wildlife, including mule deer, California condors, squirrels, and various bird species.

# 977.

The historic Grand Canyon Cemetery, located nearby, is the final resting place for early pioneers, park officials, and Native Americans.

# 978.

The village experiences a semi-arid climate, with hot summers and cool winters, and occasional snowfall.

# 979.

It is located within the ancestral lands of several Native American tribes, including the Havasupai, Hopi, Hualapai, Navajo, and Paiute.

# 980.

The South Rim, where the village is situated, offers year-round access to the Grand Canyon National Park.

# 981.

It provides a range of visitor services, including information centers, restrooms, picnic areas, and viewpoints.

## 982.

The village offers easy access to the Rim Trail, a paved pathway that stretches for miles along the canyon rim, allowing visitors to explore at their own pace.

## 983.

It is a popular destination for photography enthusiasts, providing countless opportunities to capture breathtaking landscapes and wildlife.

## 984.

The village is a starting point for various outdoor activities, such as hiking, biking, photography workshops, and helicopter tours.

## 985.

The Desert View Watchtower, located east of the village, is a historic stone tower designed by Mary Colter, offering stunning views of the canyon.

## 986.

The village has been featured in several films and documentaries, showcasing its natural beauty and cultural significance.

## 987.

It is a designated International Dark Sky Park, promoting the preservation and appreciation of dark skies and reducing light pollution.

## 988.

The village has a rich cultural heritage, with Native American influences evident in the architecture, arts, and crafts.

## 989.

It serves as a gateway to other attractions in the region, including the Navajo Nation, Horseshoe Bend, and Antelope Canyon.

## 990.

The Grand Canyon Village Historic District is listed on the National Register of Historic Places, preserving its architectural and historical significance.

## 991.

The village offers ranger-led programs and guided tours, providing educational experiences for visitors of all ages.

## 992.

It is a place of inspiration for artists, writers, and musicians, who draw inspiration from the grandeur and beauty of the canyon.

## 993.

The village is a stop on the Arizona Trail, a long-distance hiking trail spanning over 800 miles (1,287 kilometers) across the state.

## 994.

It is a haven for outdoor enthusiasts, offering opportunities for rock climbing, rafting, camping, and nature exploration.

## 995.

The Grand Canyon Village area has been inhabited by Native American tribes for thousands of years, leaving behind ancient artifacts and rock art.

## 996.

The village has a diverse workforce, with employees from various backgrounds and cultures, contributing to its vibrant atmosphere.

## 997.

It provides accessible facilities and services to accommodate visitors with disabilities, ensuring inclusivity and equal access to the natural wonders of the canyon.

## 998.

The Grand Canyon Village area has inspired numerous artists and writers, including famous painters, photographers, and authors.

## 999.

It is an important site for scientific research, with ongoing studies focusing on geology, ecology, climate change, and archaeological investigations.

## 1000.

The village has a sense of community and camaraderie, with park employees, local residents, and visitors coming together to celebrate and protect the grandeur of the Grand Canyon.